Charlie
and the
Aztecs

by Tom Jamieson

illustrated by
Clare Elsom

Introduction

The Aztecs are a group of people who lived in
Mexico hundreds of years ago.

OXFORD
UNIVERSITY PRESS
AUSTRALIA & NEW ZEALAND

OXFORD

UNIVERSITY PRESS

Oxford University Press is a department of the University of Oxford.
It furthers the University's objective of excellence in research, scholarship,
and education by publishing worldwide. Oxford is a registered trademark
of Oxford University Press in the UK and in certain other countries.

Published in Australia by
Oxford University Press
Level 8, 737 Bourke Street, Docklands, Victoria 3008, Australia

Text © Wild Pig Limited 2015, 2019
Illustrations © Clare Elsom 2015, 2019

The moral rights of the author have been asserted.

First published 2015
This edition 2019
Reprinted 2021 (twice), 2022

ISBN 9780190317690

Series Advisor: Nikki Gamble
Printed in Singapore by Markono Print Media Pte Ltd

Chapter 1

"Mum, I've finished my homework! Can I go out to play?" asked Charlie.

"All right, Charlotte. Just don't bring any more mud inside!"

Charlie always felt odd when Mum called her Charlotte.

Usually, everyone just called her Charlie.
Charlie **loved** sports.

She **loved** cricket.

She played soccer for the school team.

"I wish you were on *our* team!" said a goalie from another school.

Charlie didn't know it yet, but she was going to need all her sports skills very soon.

Chapter 2

Charlie's class was studying the Aztecs. They were visiting a museum to learn how the Aztec people lived hundreds of years ago. The museum was filled with lots of interesting objects.

Charlie's favourite object was a beautiful Aztec headdress with blue and red feathers from rainforest birds.

"Come along, class," said Mr Jones. "There's lots more to see!"

Charlie stayed behind for a closer look.

8

Charlie knew she shouldn't touch the headdress but she couldn't help herself. Carefully, she picked it up and put it on her head.

Suddenly, there was a **flash** of light.

Charlie felt her head. The headdress had gone! She looked around. The whole *museum* had gone! Birds with blue and red feathers flew overhead in the sky.

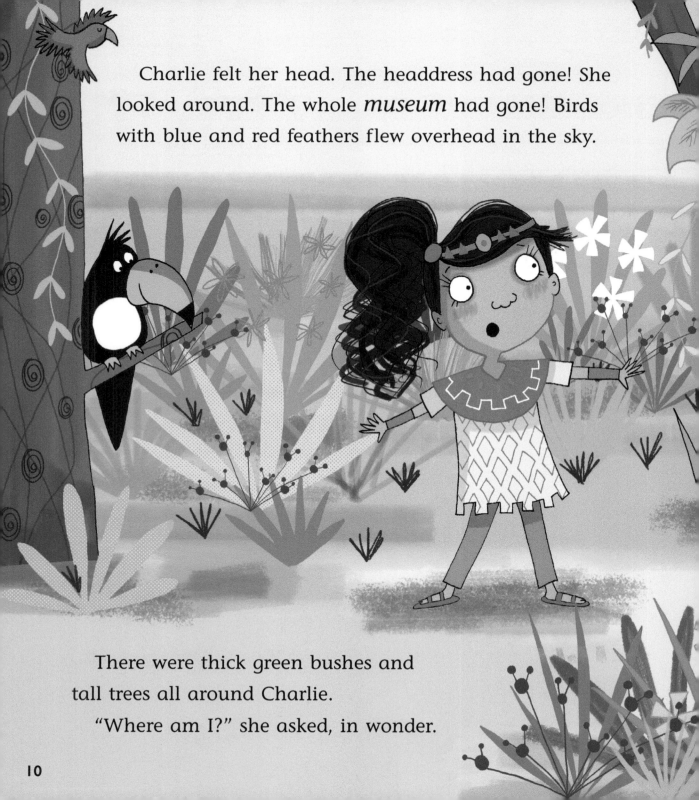

There were thick green bushes and tall trees all around Charlie.

"Where am I?" she asked, in wonder.

She was in a forest.
And not just any forest. Peering
through the bushes, Charlie could
see a village. An **Aztec** village!

"But the Aztecs lived *hundreds* of
years ago ... " said Charlie. "That
must mean ... I've travelled back
in time!"

Just then, Charlie noticed a group of boys playing.
One of the boys was pushing the others around.

"Are you new here?" said
a friendly voice behind her.
Charlie turned. It was a girl
about her age.

"Yes!" she said. "My name's Charlie."

"I'm Izel," replied the girl. "**Shh**h. I'm meant to be doing my chores … but I couldn't stay inside any longer!"

"I know just how you feel," said Charlie, grinning.

"Why is that boy being mean to the others?"
Charlie asked.

"That's Totil," said Izel. "He's the son of Zolin, our
leader. Zolin is wise and kind – but sadly, Totil is not."

"You've arrived on an important day," Izel went on.
"Once a year, we hold a sports contest to find out which
of the boys is the fittest."

"Don't the girls take part? That's silly!" said Charlie.

"I'd better get going," said Izel. "Mum needs me to collect some firewood – want to help?"

Charlie followed Izel into the forest. Izel was quick and Charlie struggled to keep up.

"Hey, you're really fast!" Charlie said.

"*You* should enter that contest."

"I'm not allowed to enter," said Izel, picking up sticks and
bits of wood. "Anyway, it's not a real contest. The other boys
always let Totil win. He says Zolin will be cross if he loses."

"If Zolin is such a wise leader, he wouldn't want anyone winning if they didn't deserve to," said Charlie.

"Yes, but Totil is his son," said Izel. "Come on, I'll race you back!"

Izel beat Charlie back to the village.

"You're too quick for me," said Charlie, panting.

They came to a line of boys who were waiting for the contest to begin.

Charlie thought for just a moment – and then joined the line!

◇·◇·◇ **Chapter 3** ◇·◇·◇

"What are you doing, Charlie?" hissed Izel. "You know girls aren't allowed in the contest!"

"No one has to know I'm a girl," said Charlie, grinning. She grabbed a helmet to hide her hair.

Izel told Charlie about the contest. It was an Aztec game called Ulama. You scored points by throwing a hard rubber ball through a stone ring.

It was just the sort of game that Charlie loved.

The crowd cheered as their leader Zolin entered the arena. He was wearing the same headdress that Charlie had tried on in the museum.

Charlie stared at the headdress. She knew she couldn't stay with the Aztecs forever. The headdress had brought her here, so maybe it could take her home?

Zolin gave the signal for the contest to begin.

Charlie watched the other boys falling over, trying to let Totil win. They looked so silly.

Totil scored two goals.

Finally, it was Charlie's turn.
She ran fast and dodged past
the boys! She took her shot.

Goal!

The crowd cheered.
Now she was just
one point behind Totil.

Charlie scored one.
Totil scored as well.
Charlie scored again.

"There's never been a game this close!"
yelled the crowd. Just then Charlie heard
the sound of a horn. **Game over!**

It was a draw.

"The winner will be decided
by a tiebreak," said Zolin.
"You both get one shot."

Totil went first.

He missed!

If Charlie scored, she would win.
"Please Charlie, miss!" said Izel under her breath.

Chapter 4

"Maybe I should let Totil win," thought Charlie, as she lined up her shot.

No, she couldn't do that.

Her ball flew straight through the ring. Charlie had won! The crowd cheered.

Zolin stepped forward, looking stern. Suddenly, Charlie felt very scared.

"We've never seen a boy beat my son before," he said.

"Well," said Charlie bravely, "My name is Charlie, and I'm a girl!" She took off her helmet.

"Girls aren't allowed to play!" screeched Totil. "It's against the rules.

I win!"

"Not so fast," said Zolin, calmly. "Charlie won fair and square. She is the winner."

He really was a wise leader.

Totil sulked, while Izel hugged Charlie.

"Next year, I'm going to enter!" Izel said.

The crowd cheered.

"I will grant you one favour, Charlie," said Zolin.

"Can I … try on your headdress?" asked Charlie.

Zolin looked puzzled, but smiled. He carefully handed Charlie the headdress.

"Thank you," she said. She put it on and crossed her fingers …

Once again, there was a flash of light!

Suddenly, Charlie was back in the museum. The headdress was back on its stand.

"**Hurry up, Charlie!**" called Mr Jones.

"I'm back! Everything's back, just the way it was ... " said Charlie, looking around happily.

"Or maybe not!" she said, spotting a painting on the wall. It showed Izel – and she was playing Ulama!